Open Letter To My Child's Father

Designed
by
S.H Bando Press

www.shbandopress.com
Questions And Customer Service:
email us at contact@shbandopress.com

Disclaimer Notes

This Journal Belongs To

....

The Window by Rumi

Your body is away
from me.
but there is a
window open.
from my heart to
yours.
From this window
like the moon.
I keep sending
news secretly.

Dear Husband, I want to Say

I can bear much more than you think, but I need _____

_____

_____

_____

_____

I really wish that _____

_____

_____

_____

_____

_____

Life without you is _____

_____

_____

_____

_____

_____

_____

Since you've been gone, I find it difficult to _____

_____

_____

_____

_____

_____

I will be patient _____

_____

_____

Because _____

_____

_____

_____

Now that you are gone I feel _____

_____

_____

_____

_____

To allow these feelings room to transform into something else, I am willing to _____

_____

_____

_____

_____

I am ready to feel _____

_____

_____

_____

_____

_____

_____

One way I can express this feeling in a creative way
is _____

_____
_____
_____
_____

Whenever I start to feel overwhelmed by pain, regret -
guilt, or despair, I will repeat this mantra _____

_____
_____
_____
_____

To be more compassionate toward myself, I am willing to
try _____

_____
_____
_____
_____

There someone else who is hurting, like _____
_____ and , _____

I could do _____
_____

to show them I care and _____
_____
_____

My Favourite Memories With My Husband Is

_____

_____
_____
_____
_____
_____
_____
_____
_____
_____
_____
_____
_____
_____
_____
_____
_____
_____
_____
_____
_____
_____
_____
_____
_____

Things That Will Always Remind Me Of My Husband {Images – Songs – Scents _ Food – Quotes – and more}

Redemption Song by
Kevin Young

Grief might be easy
if there wasn't still
such beauty – would
be far
simpler if the silver
maple didn't thrust
its leaves into
flame

Dear Husband

I know I'm going to be okay because _____

_____

_____

_____

_____

A simple activity I could try in this period to make things easier is _____

_____

_____

_____

_____

_____

I could use some more _____

_____

_____

_____

_____

_____

I could use a little less _____

_____

_____

_____

_____

Since you are gone, I'm going to _____

_____

_____

_____

My 'forward motion' plan for this month _____

_____

_____

_____

_____

_____

My 'forward motion' plan for this year _____

_____

_____

_____

_____

_____

I will depend on _____

_____

_____

_____

_____

_____

How things have changed _____
_____
_____
_____
_____
_____

When I wake up in the morning _____
_____
_____
_____
_____
_____
_____

When I do things like _____
_____
_____
_____

I think of you _____
_____
_____
_____

If I could tell you one thing _____
_____
_____
_____

My Favourite Memories With My Husband Is

_____

_____

_____

_____

_____

_____

_____

_____

_____

_____

_____

_____

_____

_____

_____

_____

_____

_____

_____

_____

_____

_____

Things That Will Always Remind Me Of My Husband {Images - Songs - Scents _ Food - Quotes - and more}

''Faraway''
Poetry

After you left
nothing made
any sense: it felt like
the world was ending
yet the sun kept
rising
day after day.

Dear Husband

After (insert what happened) _____
_____

_____
_____
_____
_____

I felt _____
_____
_____

I never wanted _____
_____
_____
_____
_____
_____

I'm angry that _____
_____
_____
_____
_____

I wish I could have told you _____
_____

_____
_____
_____

What I miss the most is _____

_____
_____
_____
_____
_____

I choose to remember you by _____

_____
_____
_____
_____
_____
_____

Every time I see _____

_____
_____
_____
_____
_____
_____ I think of you

If you were here now _____

_____
_____
_____

_____
_____
_____

How I felt when I was around you _____

_____

_____

_____

_____

My favorite thing we used to do together _____

_____

_____

_____

_____

_____

Today I remembered _____

_____

_____

_____

_____

_____

Our favorite places _____

_____

_____

_____

_____

My Favourite Memories With My Husband Is

Things That Will Always Remind Me Of My Husband {Images - Songs - Scents _ Food - Quotes - and more}

''Faith smith''
Poetry

The sky cried with
me today.
I let the rain come
down hard
over me and felt you
in every drop.
It's as if even the
heavens
know you belong on
Earth.

Dear Husband

Things you taught me about myself _____

_____

_____

_____

Ten words that best describe you _____

- _____
- _____
- _____
- _____
- _____
- _____
- _____
- _____
- _____
- _____

My favorite quote that sums you up _____

_____

_____

_____

_____

_____

_____

If I could be like you in any way, I would adopt their

_____

_____

_____

_____

_____

Your best quality _____

_____

_____

_____

_____

_____

Your worst quality _____

_____

_____

_____

_____

_____

Things you hated _____

_____

_____

_____

_____

_____

Things you loved _____
_____
_____
_____
_____
_____

This quote reminds me of you _____
_____
_____
_____
_____
_____

_____ when you told me that
The kind things people say _____
_____
_____
_____
_____

I will like to express my gratitude _____
_____
_____
_____
_____

My Favourite Memories With My Husband Is

_____

_____
_____
_____
_____
_____
_____
_____
_____
_____
_____
_____
_____
_____
_____
_____
_____
_____
_____
_____
_____
_____
_____
_____
_____

Things That Will Always Remind Me Of My Husband {Images – Songs – Scents _ Food – Quotes – and more}

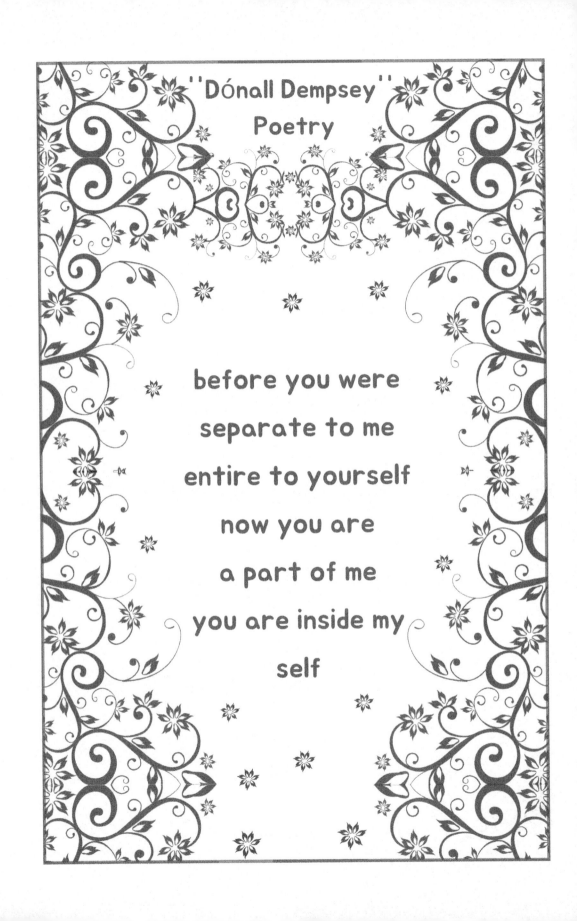

"Dónall Dempsey"
Poetry

before you were

separate to me

entire to yourself

now you are

a part of me

you are inside my

self

Dear Husband

If I could change one thing ,it would be _____
_____
_____
_____
_____
_____

Ten Things I've learned about myself since you passed
away _____
- _____
- _____
- _____
- _____
- _____
- _____
- _____
- _____
- _____
- _____

I am having a hard time with _____
_____
_____
_____
_____
_____

The hardest time of day is _____

_____

_____

_____

_____

In the last days, I have been feeling a lot of _____

_____

_____

_____

_____

_____

_____

How I will continue coping every day _____

_____

_____

_____

_____

_____

My support system is _____

_____

_____

_____

_____

_____

_____

My support system includes too ——————————

- ——————————————————————
- ——————————————————————
- ——————————————————————
- ——————————————————————
- ——————————————————————
- ——————————————————————

A tradition that helps me remember ——————

———————————————————————
———————————————————————
———————————————————————
———————————————————————
———————————————————————

The little things that meant a lot ——————

———————————————————————
———————————————————————
———————————————————————
———————————————————————
———————————————————————
———————————————————————

I wish someone would say ——————————

———————————————————————
———————————————————————
———————————————————————
———————————————————————

My Favourite Memories With My Husband Is

_____

_____

_____

_____

_____

_____

_____

_____

_____

_____

_____

_____

_____

_____

_____

_____

_____

_____

_____

_____

_____

_____

Your last words to me _____

_____

_____

_____

_____

_____

_____

_____

_____

Dear Husband, you are always in my heart _____

_____

_____

_____

_____

_____

_____

_____

_____

_____

_____

_____

_____

_____

Things That Will Always Remind Me Of My Husband {Images - Songs - Scents _ Food - Quotes - and more}

At last, give yourself time to grieve, everyone grieves differently and within their own timeframe, hopefully, some of the changes are eventual decreases in the intensity of painful feelings and longing and decreases in the length of time grief and feel overwhelming, the low times aren't as low and don't last as long, As time passes and we grow, we can also have new questions and insights about our losses which change the grief we experience, just let your heart and mind heal from this traumatic experience, never judge yourself in the healing process. whenever needed, just write again freely.

	Yes	No
Do I feel much better	☐	☐
Do I recommend this journal	☐	☐
Does it deserve a good review	☐	☐

Made in the USA
Middletown, DE
06 October 2023

40358487R00027